G.W.

Embrace Your Value

A Journey to Self-Worth

"You yourself, as much as anybody in the entire universe, deserve your love and affection."

— Buddha

Contents

1

Understanding Self-Worth

D*efining Self-Worth*

Understanding the Concept

- Self-worth refers to the value and significance one assigns to oneself.
  - It encompasses a deep sense of self-respect, self-acceptance, and self-esteem.
  - Unlike self-esteem, which may fluctuate based on external validation, self-worth is intrinsic and stable.

Components of Self-Worth

- Self-Acceptance: Acknowledging and embracing all aspects of oneself, including strengths, weaknesses, flaws, and imperfections.
- Self-Respect: Treating oneself with kindness, dignity, and compassion, regardless of external circumstances or others' opinions.
- Self-Value: Recognizing one's inherent worthiness as a human being, independent of achievements, possessions, or social status.

Sources of Self-Worth

- Internal Validation: Relying on personal beliefs, values, and accomplishments to derive a sense of worthiness.
- External Validation: Seeking approval, praise, or validation from others as a basis for self-worth, which can be unreliable and fleeting.
- Comparison: Measuring one's worth against others, often leading to feelings of inadequacy or superiority.

Impact of Self-Worth on Well-Being

- Mental Health: Low self-worth is associated with conditions such as depression, anxiety, and low self-esteem, while high self-worth promotes psychological resilience and well-being.
- Relationships: Healthy self-worth fosters fulfilling relationships based on mutual respect and authenticity, whereas low self-worth may lead to dependency, insecurity, or codependency.
- Achievement and Success: Believing in one's abilities and worthiness enhances motivation, perseverance, and goal attainment, whereas self-doubt and insecurity may hinder progress.

Cultivating Self-Worth

- Self-Reflection: Examining beliefs, attitudes, and behaviors that contribute to self-worth.
- Self-Compassion: Practicing kindness, forgiveness, and understanding towards oneself, especially during times of difficulty or failure.
- Personal Growth: Engaging in activities that promote self-awareness, self-improvement, and self-empowerment.
- Positive Relationships: Surrounding oneself with supportive indi-

viduals who affirm and appreciate one's worth.
- Setting Boundaries: Establishing healthy boundaries to protect one's self-esteem and well-being from negative influences.

Understanding self-worth is essential for fostering a positive self-concept and leading a fulfilling life. By recognizing and embracing their intrinsic value, individuals can cultivate resilience, authenticity, and a greater sense of fulfillment in their personal and interpersonal experiences.

Exploring the Connection Between Self-Worth and Mental Health

Self-Worth as a Foundation for Mental Health

- Sense of Value: A strong sense of self-worth provides individuals with a foundation of self-value and self-respect, which are crucial for mental well-being.
- Resilience: High self-worth acts as a buffer against stress, adversity, and negative life events, contributing to greater resilience in coping with challenges.
- Self-Efficacy: Believing in one's capabilities and worthiness enhances self-efficacy, the belief in one's ability to achieve goals and overcome obstacles, which is vital for mental health.

Impact of Low Self-Worth on Mental Health

- Depression and Anxiety: Low self-worth is closely linked to conditions such as depression and anxiety, as individuals may experience feelings of worthlessness, inadequacy, or hopelessness.
- Negative Self-Talk: Persistent negative self-talk, characterized by self-criticism and self-doubt, contributes to the development and

maintenance of mental health disorders.

- <u>Perfectionism</u>: Striving for unrealistic standards and fearing failure can exacerbate feelings of low self-worth and lead to increased stress and anxiety.

Relationship Dynamics

- <u>Codependency</u>: Individuals with low self-worth may engage in codependent relationships, seeking validation and approval from others to fill the void of self-worth, which can perpetuate unhealthy relationship dynamics.
- <u>Boundaries</u>: Poor self-worth often leads to difficulties in setting and maintaining healthy boundaries, which can result in interpersonal conflicts, resentment, and further stress.

Healing and Recovery

- <u>Therapeutic Interventions</u>: Therapy, including cognitive-behavioral therapy (CBT), dialectical behavior therapy (DBT), and acceptance and commitment therapy (ACT), can help individuals address underlying issues contributing to low self-worth and develop healthier self-concepts.
- <u>Self-Compassion Practices</u>: Cultivating self-compassion, through mindfulness, self-care, and self-acceptance exercises, fosters resilience, self-esteem, and emotional well-being.
- <u>Building Support Networks</u>: Surrounding oneself with supportive individuals who affirm and appreciate one's worth can provide validation and encouragement in the healing process.

Promoting Positive Self-Worth

- <u>Positive Affirmations</u>: Practicing positive affirmations and self-talk can reframe negative beliefs and reinforce a sense of self-worth.
- <u>Identifying Strengths</u>: Recognizing and celebrating personal strengths, achievements, and talents enhances self-esteem and fosters a positive self-concept.
- <u>Self-Expression</u>: Engaging in activities that promote self-expression, creativity, and authenticity nurtures a sense of identity and belonging.

Understanding the intricate relationship between self-worth and mental health is crucial for promoting psychological well-being and resilience. By addressing underlying issues related to self-worth and fostering self-compassion and self-acceptance, individuals can embark on a journey towards improved mental health and overall life satisfaction.

Recognizing Signs of Low Self-Worth

Recognizing signs of low self-worth is an important step towards addressing and improving one's self-esteem. *Here are some common signs:*

Self-Criticism: Constantly berating oneself for perceived flaws or mistakes, often accompanied by negative self-talk.

Perfectionism: Setting unrealistically high standards for oneself and feeling inadequate or worthless when unable to meet them.

Approval-Seeking Behavior: Constantly seeking validation and approval from others to feel worthy or accepted.

Difficulty Accepting Compliments: Feeling uncomfortable or dismissing compliments, as they don't align with one's low self-image.

Comparison: Constantly comparing oneself unfavorably to others, leading to feelings of inferiority or envy.

Avoidance of Challenges: Avoiding new experiences or challenges due to fear of failure or inadequacy.

Negative Body Image: Feeling dissatisfied or ashamed of one's appearance, regardless of actual physical characteristics.

Difficulty Asserting Boundaries: Struggling to assert boundaries or say no to others, prioritizing their needs over one's own.

Self-Isolation: Withdrawing from social interactions or activities due to feelings of unworthiness or fear of rejection.

Dependence on External Validation: Relying heavily on external validation or achievements to feel worthy or valuable.

Pessimism: Adopting a negative outlook on life and expecting failure or disappointment in various aspects of life.

Feeling Unworthy of Love or Happiness: Believing oneself to be undeserving of love, happiness, or success.

Recognizing these signs is the first step towards addressing low self-worth. By acknowledging these patterns and seeking support, individuals can begin to challenge negative beliefs and cultivate a healthier sense of self-esteem and self-worth.

2

Identifying Limiting Beliefs

ncovering Negative Self-Talk

Uncovering negative self-talk is a crucial step in improving self-worth and promoting a more positive self-image. *Here's how to recognize and address negative self-talk:*

Awareness: Begin by becoming aware of your inner dialogue. Pay attention to the thoughts and messages you tell yourself throughout the day, especially during challenging or stressful situations.

Identify Patterns: Notice recurring themes or patterns in your negative self-talk. These may include self-criticism, doubt, fear of failure, or harsh judgments about your abilities or worth.

External Triggers: Identify situations or triggers that tend to amplify negative self-talk. These could be specific people, environments, or events that evoke feelings of insecurity or inadequacy.

Challenge Negative Beliefs: Question the validity of your negative thoughts. Ask yourself if there is evidence to support these beliefs or if they are based on assumptions or past experiences.

Cognitive Restructuring: Practice replacing negative thoughts with more realistic and compassionate ones. Challenge negative statements with affirmations or counterarguments that promote self-compassion and self-acceptance.

Practice Self-Compassion: Treat yourself with the same kindness and understanding you would offer to a friend facing similar challenges. Practice self-compassion exercises, such as self-soothing techniques or writing yourself a supportive letter.

Reframe Negative Thoughts: Reframe negative thoughts into more positive or neutral statements. Instead of saying, "I'm a failure," reframe it as, "I'm learning and growing from this experience."

Mindfulness: Use mindfulness techniques to observe your thoughts without judgment. Notice when negative self-talk arises and gently redirect your attention to the present moment or more positive aspects of yourself.

Seek Support: Share your struggles with trusted friends, family members, or a therapist. Talking about your negative self-talk can help bring it into perspective and provide support in challenging and reframing these thoughts.

Practice Self-Care: Engage in activities that promote self-care and self-compassion, such as exercise, hobbies, relaxation techniques, or spending time with supportive loved ones.

By uncovering and challenging negative self-talk, you can begin to cultivate a more compassionate and empowering inner dialogue, leading to improved self-esteem and a stronger sense of self-worth.

Examining Childhood Influences on Self-Worth

Examining childhood influences on self-worth is essential for understanding how early experiences shape our beliefs about ourselves. *Here's how childhood experiences can impact self-worth:*

Parental Influence

- Parenting Style: Authoritative, nurturing parenting tends to promote healthy self-esteem, while authoritarian or neglectful parenting may contribute to low self-worth.
- Parental Feedback: Positive reinforcement and encouragement from caregivers can boost self-esteem, while criticism or neglect can undermine it.
- Attachment: Secure attachment to caregivers during infancy and childhood lays the foundation for a positive self-concept and healthy self-worth.

Family Dynamics

- Siblings and Peers: Relationships with siblings and peers can influence self-worth through comparisons, social acceptance, and validation.
- Family Environment: Growing up in a supportive, nurturing family environment fosters a sense of belonging and self-worth, while a dysfunctional or abusive family environment can erode it.

School and Social Environment

- Academic Achievement: Success or failure in school can impact self-worth, with consistent academic praise boosting confidence and repeated failure undermining it.
- Bullying or Peer Rejection: Negative experiences such as bullying or social rejection can have lasting effects on self-esteem and self-worth.

Cultural and Societal Influences

- Cultural Expectations: Cultural norms and expectations regarding success, appearance, and behavior shape beliefs about self-worth.
- Media Influence: Media portrayals of beauty, success, and happiness can contribute to unrealistic standards and comparisons, affecting self-worth.

Trauma and Adversity

- Early Trauma: Childhood trauma, such as abuse, neglect, or loss, can profoundly impact self-worth and contribute to feelings of worthlessness, shame, or inadequacy.
- Adversity: Adverse childhood experiences, such as poverty, instability, or parental divorce, can challenge self-esteem and resilience.

Internalization of Beliefs

- Internalized Messages: Beliefs and messages internalized during childhood, whether positive or negative, shape the way individuals perceive themselves and their worth.
- Core Beliefs: Core beliefs formed in childhood influence self-worth

throughout life, unless consciously examined and challenged.

Resilience and Coping Strategies

- <u>Protective Factors</u>: Supportive relationships, positive role models, and resilience-building experiences can mitigate the impact of adverse childhood experiences on self-worth.
- <u>Coping Mechanisms</u>: Individuals develop coping mechanisms in response to childhood experiences, which can either support or hinder self-worth development.

Examining childhood influences on self-worth provides insight into the origins of beliefs about oneself and offers opportunities for healing, growth, and empowerment. By understanding how early experiences shape self-worth, individuals can work towards cultivating a more positive and resilient sense of self-esteem.

Recognizing and Challenging Limiting Beliefs

Recognizing and challenging limiting beliefs is a crucial step in improving self-worth and fostering personal growth. *Here's how to identify and address them effectively:*

Recognizing Limiting Beliefs

Self-Awareness: Pay attention to your thoughts, especially in situations where you feel insecure or doubtful. Notice recurring themes or patterns in your inner dialogue.

Emotional Responses: Identify the emotions associated with your thoughts. Limiting beliefs often evoke feelings of fear, shame, guilt, or inadequacy.

Behavioral Patterns: Notice how limiting beliefs influence your behavior. Do they hold you back from pursuing opportunities, taking risks, or expressing yourself authentically?

Triggers: Identify situations or triggers that activate your limiting beliefs. These could be specific events, people, or environments that reinforce negative self-perceptions.

Negative Self-Talk: Pay attention to the language you use when talking to yourself. Notice if your inner dialogue is critical, judgmental, or defeatist.

Challenging Limiting Beliefs

Question the Evidence: Challenge the validity of your limiting beliefs by examining the evidence supporting them. Ask yourself if there are alternative interpretations or counterexamples that contradict your beliefs.

Reality Testing: Test your assumptions and beliefs by gathering objective information or seeking feedback from others. This can help you gain a more accurate perspective on yourself and your abilities.

Reframe Negative Thoughts: Replace negative thoughts with more realistic and empowering alternatives. Reframe self-defeating statements into affirmations or statements of self-compassion and resilience.

Examine Origins: Explore the origins of your limiting beliefs. Consider whether they stem from past experiences, societal messages, or internalized beliefs from childhood.

Challenge Distortions: Identify cognitive distortions such as black-and-white thinking, catastrophizing, or personalization that contribute to your limiting beliefs. Challenge these distortions with more balanced and rational perspectives.

Practice Self-Compassion: Treat yourself with kindness and understanding as you challenge your limiting beliefs. Offer yourself the same compassion and support you would give to a friend facing similar struggles.

Set Realistic Goals: Break down your goals into manageable steps and set realistic expectations for yourself. Celebrate your progress and accomplishments along the way, no matter how small.

Seek Support: Reach out to friends, family members, or a therapist for support and encouragement. Sharing your struggles with others can provide valuable perspective and validation.

By recognizing and challenging limiting beliefs, you can break free from self-imposed barriers and cultivate a more positive and empowering mindset. With practice and persistence, you can transform your self-perceptions and cultivate greater self-worth and resilience.

3

Cultivating Self-Compassion

nderstanding the Role of Self-Compassion in Building Self-Worth

Understanding the role of self-compassion in building self-worth is essential for cultivating a positive self-image and nurturing emotional well-being. *Here's how self-compassion contributes to building self-worth:*

Acknowledging Imperfection: Self-compassion involves recognizing and accepting one's imperfections, shortcomings, and mistakes with kindness and understanding. Rather than harsh self-criticism, individuals approach themselves with empathy and forgiveness.

Validation of Emotions: Self-compassion validates the full range of human emotions, including those that may be difficult or uncomfortable. Instead of denying or suppressing emotions, individuals acknowledge their feelings with compassion and non-judgment.

Cultivating Self-Acceptance: Self-compassion fosters a sense of self-acceptance and unconditional self-worth. Individuals learn to embrace themselves as they are, with all their strengths and weaknesses, without needing to meet unrealistic standards or conditions.

Nurturing Inner Support: Self-compassion provides inner support and reassurance during times of struggle or distress. Individuals become their own source of comfort and encouragement, offering themselves the care and kindness they need to navigate life's challenges.

Reducing Self-Criticism: Self-compassion helps to counteract self-criticism and negative self-talk. By replacing self-judgment with self-kindness, individuals cultivate a more supportive and nurturing inner dialogue, promoting feelings of worthiness and self-esteem.

Fostering Resilience: Self-compassion contributes to resilience by buffering against the impact of stress, setbacks, and failures. Individuals with self-compassion are better able to bounce back from difficulties, learning and growing from their experiences without undue self-blame or shame.

Promoting Self-Care: Self-compassion encourages individuals to prioritize their well-being and self-care. Rather than neglecting their needs or overextending themselves to please others, individuals practice self-care as an expression of self-compassion and self-respect.

Enhancing Interpersonal Relationships: Self-compassion positively influences interpersonal relationships by fostering empathy, under-standing, and compassion towards others. When individuals are kinder and more accepting of themselves, they are better able to extend the same kindness and acceptance to others, deepening their connections and sense of belonging.

Encouraging Growth Mindset: Self-compassion nurtures a growth mindset by promoting a sense of curiosity, openness, and resilience in the face of challenges. Individuals with self-compassion view failures and setbacks as opportunities for learning and growth, rather than reflections of their worth or abilities.

In summary, self-compassion plays a vital role in building self-worth by fostering self-acceptance, reducing self-criticism, promoting resilience, and nurturing emotional well-being. By cultivating self-compassion, individuals can develop a more positive and compassionate relationship with themselves, leading to greater self-worth and overall life satisfaction.

Practicing Self-Compassion Exercises

Here are some self-compassion exercises that you can practice to cultivate kindness, understanding, and acceptance towards yourself:

Self-Compassionate Letter Writing

- Write a letter to yourself from the perspective of a compassionate friend.
- Express understanding, kindness, and support for yourself, acknowledging your struggles and offering words of encouragement and reassurance.
- Read the letter aloud to yourself with a gentle and compassionate tone.

Self-Compassion Break

- Take a moment to pause and acknowledge your current experience, whether it's a difficult emotion, physical discomfort, or challenging situation.

- Say to yourself, "This is a moment of suffering. Suffering is a part of life."
- Offer yourself words of kindness and understanding, such as "May I be kind to myself in this moment," or "May I give myself the compassion I need."

Self-Compassionate Touch

- Place your hand over your heart or gently hold your own hand.
- Close your eyes and connect with the warmth and comfort of your touch.
- Offer yourself words of kindness and support, such as "I am here for you," or "You are worthy of love and compassion."

Common Humanity Meditation

- Sit comfortably and take a few deep breaths to center yourself.
- Reflect on the shared human experience of suffering, acknowledging that you are not alone in your struggles.
- Repeat a phrase such as "May I remember that I am not alone in my suffering. Others also experience pain and difficulties."

Self-Compassion Journaling

- Set aside time each day to write in a journal about your experiences, emotions, and thoughts.
- Practice self-compassion by acknowledging your feelings without judgment and offering yourself words of kindness and understanding.

- Reflect on moments of self-compassion and moments when you could have been more gentle and supportive towards yourself.

Self-Compassion Affirmations

- Create a list of self-compassionate affirmations or phrases that resonate with you.
- Repeat these affirmations to yourself throughout the day, especially during moments of self-doubt or criticism.
- Examples include "I am worthy of love and kindness," "I accept myself as I am," and "I forgive myself for my mistakes."

Self-Compassionate Visualization

- Close your eyes and imagine yourself surrounded by a warm, soothing light.
- Visualize yourself wrapped in a comforting embrace, feeling safe, loved, and accepted.
- Allow yourself to experience the feelings of kindness, compassion, and acceptance flowing towards you.

Practicing these self-compassion exercises regularly can help you develop a more compassionate and nurturing relationship with yourself, fostering greater self-worth and emotional well-being. Remember to be patient and gentle with yourself as you explore these practices.

Overcoming Perfectionism and Self-Criticism

Overcoming perfectionism and self-criticism is essential for cultivating self-worth and promoting emotional well-being. *Here are some strategies to help you break free from these patterns:*

Challenge All-or-Nothing Thinking

- Recognize that perfectionism often stems from all-or-nothing thinking, where success is equated with flawlessness.
- Challenge this mindset by embracing the idea that mistakes and imperfections are a natural part of the learning process.

Set Realistic Goals

- Set goals that are challenging yet attainable, allowing room for mistakes and setbacks.
- Break larger goals into smaller, more manageable tasks, and celebrate progress along the way.

Practice Self-Compassion

- Treat yourself with kindness and understanding, especially when facing challenges or setbacks.
- Practice self-compassion exercises, such as self-soothing techniques, positive self-talk, and self-care activities.

Reframe Failure as Learning

- Shift your perspective on failure from something to be feared or avoided to an opportunity for growth and learning.
- Reflect on what you can learn from mistakes and setbacks, and use them as valuable lessons for future improvement.

Challenge Perfectionistic Standards

- Question the unrealistic standards you set for yourself and the sources of these standards, such as societal pressure or internalized beliefs.

- Set more flexible and compassionate standards that allow for mistakes and imperfections.

Practice Mindfulness

- Cultivate mindfulness to observe your thoughts and emotions without judgment.
- Notice when self-critical thoughts arise and gently redirect your attention to the present moment or more constructive perspectives.

Celebrate Progress, Not Perfection

- Focus on progress rather than perfection, acknowledging your efforts and achievements along the way.
- Celebrate small wins and milestones, no matter how insignificant they may seem.

Seek Support

- Reach out to friends, family members, or a therapist for support and encouragement.
- Share your struggles with perfectionism and self-criticism, and seek guidance on developing healthier coping strategies.

Practice Self-Validation

- Validate your own worth and accomplishments, rather than seeking external validation or approval.
- Remind yourself of your strengths, talents, and unique qualities,

affirming your inherent worthiness.

Set Boundaries

- Establish boundaries to protect yourself from perfectionistic tendencies and self-critical thoughts.
- Recognize when you need to step back, take breaks, or delegate tasks to maintain balance and well-being.

Overcoming perfectionism and self-criticism takes time and practice, but with persistence and self-compassion, you can cultivate a healthier relationship with yourself and experience greater self-worth and fulfillment.

4

Discovering Your Strengths

I *dentifying Personal Strengths and Talents*

Identifying personal strengths and talents is a powerful way to build self-worth and confidence. *Here's how you can discover and acknowledge your unique abilities:*

Self-Reflection

- Take time to reflect on your past experiences, accomplishments, and challenges.
- Consider the tasks or activities that come naturally to you and those that you enjoy doing.

Feedback from Others

- Seek feedback from friends, family, colleagues, and mentors about your strengths and talents.
- Ask others what they see as your most notable qualities or skills.

Strengths Assessment Tools

- Use strengths assessment tools such as the VIA Survey of Character Strengths or the StrengthsFinder assessment to identify your top strengths.
- These assessments can provide valuable insights into your unique qualities and talents.

Journaling

- Keep a journal where you write about your achievements, moments of success, and instances where you felt particularly capable or confident.
- Reflect on the skills and qualities that contributed to those successes.

Explore Different Activities

- Engage in a variety of activities and hobbies to discover your interests and talents.
- Pay attention to activities that energize you and bring you joy, as these often indicate areas of strength.

Ask Yourself Questions

Ask yourself questions such as:

- What am I naturally good at?
- What activities do I find effortless or enjoyable?
- When do I feel most confident and competent?
- What accomplishments am I proud of?

- What positive feedback have I received from others?

Observe Your Reactions

- Pay attention to how you react in different situations and environments.
- Notice when you feel confident, capable, or in your element, as these moments often reveal your strengths.

Seek Patterns

- Look for patterns or themes in your strengths and talents.
- Identify commonalities among different areas where you excel, such as leadership, creativity, problem-solving, or empathy.

Experiment and Challenge Yourself

- Step out of your comfort zone and try new things.
- Take on challenges that allow you to stretch and develop your skills, uncovering hidden talents in the process.

Celebrate Your Achievements

- Acknowledge and celebrate your achievements, no matter how small.
- Recognize the effort and dedication you put into reaching your goals, affirming your capabilities and worthiness.

By actively exploring and acknowledging your personal strengths and talents, you can cultivate a greater sense of self-awareness, confidence, and self-worth. Embrace your unique qualities and use them to navigate life's challenges and pursue your passions with purpose and authenticity.

Exploring Past Achievements and Successes

Exploring past achievements and successes is a valuable way to recognize your capabilities, strengths, and areas of expertise. *Here's how you can reflect on and explore your past accomplishments:*

Make a List

- Start by making a list of your past achievements and successes, both big and small.
- Include academic achievements, career milestones, personal accomplishments, and any other moments of success you can recall.

Reflect on Challenges Overcome

- Consider the challenges or obstacles you've faced in the past and how you overcame them.
- Reflect on the skills, qualities, and strategies you utilized to navigate those challenges successfully.

Identify Patterns and Themes

- Look for patterns or themes among your past achievements.
- Identify common skills, strengths, or qualities that contributed to your success in different areas of your life.

Consider Feedback and Recognition

- Think about any feedback, praise, or recognition you've received from others for your accomplishments.

- Consider the qualities or skills that others have acknowledged and appreciated in you.

Review Work and Project History

- Review your work history and past projects to remind yourself of the contributions you've made.
- Reflect on the impact of your work and the value you've added to organizations or teams.

Think Beyond Work and Academics

- Don't limit your exploration to professional or academic achievements.
- Consider personal achievements, such as relationships nurtured, personal goals achieved, or challenges overcome outside of work or school.

Journaling

- Keep a journal where you write about your past achievements and successes.
- Reflect on how these experiences have shaped you and contributed to your growth and development.

Visualize Your Successes

- Visualize yourself achieving success in past situations.
- Recall the feelings of pride, satisfaction, and accomplishment associated with those moments.

Share Stories with Others

- Share stories of your past achievements and successes with friends, family, or mentors.
- Discuss the lessons learned and insights gained from those experiences.

Celebrate Your Accomplishments

- Take time to celebrate your past accomplishments and successes.
- Acknowledge the effort, perseverance, and dedication that went into achieving those goals.

By exploring your past achievements and successes, you can gain a deeper understanding of your strengths, capabilities, and areas of expertise. Use these reflections to build confidence, set future goals, and continue striving for success in all areas of your life.

Harnessing Your Strengths to Boost Self-Worth

Harnessing your strengths to boost self-worth involves leveraging your unique qualities and capabilities to cultivate a greater sense of confidence, accomplishment, and fulfillment. *Here's how you can effectively utilize your strengths to enhance your self-worth:*

Identify Your Strengths

- Reflect on your skills, talents, and qualities that you excel in or enjoy using.
- Consider feedback from others, past achievements, and moments of flow or engagement as indicators of your strengths.

Set Goals Aligned with Your Strengths

- Define goals that align with your strengths and interests, allowing you to leverage your natural abilities to achieve success.
- Focus on activities and projects that allow you to utilize and develop your strengths further.

Build on Your Strengths

- Continuously work to develop and enhance your strengths through practice, learning, and experience.
- Seek out opportunities for growth and skill development that align with your areas of strength.

Apply Your Strengths in Various Areas of Your Life

- Look for opportunities to apply your strengths in different domains, including work, relationships, hobbies, and personal development.
- Use your strengths to overcome challenges, solve problems, and achieve your goals in various aspects of your life.

Celebrate Your Successes

- Acknowledge and celebrate your successes and achievements that result from utilizing your strengths.
- Take pride in your abilities and the positive impact they have on your life and the lives of others.

Accept and Embrace Your Uniqueness

- Embrace your unique combination of strengths, recognizing that everyone has their own set of talents and abilities.

- Avoid comparing yourself to others and focus on developing and maximizing your own strengths.

Express Gratitude for Your Strengths

- Practice gratitude for the strengths and talents you possess, recognizing them as valuable assets that contribute to your well-being and success.
- Express appreciation for your abilities and the opportunities they provide.

Use Your Strengths to Help Others

- Share your strengths with others by offering support, guidance, and assistance based on your areas of expertise.
- Use your strengths to make a positive difference in the lives of those around you, enhancing your sense of purpose and fulfillment.

Challenge Yourself

- Step outside your comfort zone and challenge yourself to apply your strengths in new and unfamiliar situations.
- Embrace opportunities for growth and development that allow you to stretch and expand your capabilities.

Practice Self-Reflection

- Regularly reflect on how you're using your strengths and the impact they're having on your life.
- Identify areas where you can further leverage your strengths and

opportunities for growth.

By harnessing your strengths and using them intentionally to achieve your goals and make a positive impact, you can enhance your self-worth and cultivate a greater sense of confidence, purpose, and fulfillment in your life.

5

Setting Healthy Boundaries

*U*nderstanding *the Importance of Boundaries in Self-Worth*

Understanding the importance of boundaries in self-worth is crucial for maintaining healthy relationships, preserving personal well-being, and fostering a sense of autonomy and respect. *Here's how boundaries contribute to self-worth:*

Preserving Self-Respect

- Boundaries serve as a reflection of self-respect and self-worth, signaling to others how you expect to be treated.
- By setting and enforcing boundaries, you communicate your inherent value and worthiness of respect and consideration.

Protecting Emotional Health

- Boundaries help protect your emotional well-being by establishing limits on what you're willing to accept or tolerate in relationships and interactions.

- They prevent others from infringing upon your feelings, needs, and boundaries, reducing the risk of emotional harm or manipulation.

Asserting Personal Autonomy

- Boundaries empower you to assert your autonomy and individuality, allowing you to make choices and decisions that align with your values, preferences, and goals.
- They reinforce your sense of agency and control over your own life, enhancing feelings of self-efficacy and empowerment.

Establishing Healthy Relationships

- Healthy boundaries are essential for fostering mutually respectful and fulfilling relationships.
- They create a framework for clear communication, mutual understanding, and respect for each other's needs and boundaries, contributing to relationship satisfaction and longevity.

Preventing Resentment and Burnout

- Setting boundaries helps prevent feelings of resentment, overwhelm, and burnout by managing expectations and workload effectively.
- By honoring your limits and prioritizing self-care, you preserve your energy and well-being, reducing the risk of emotional exhaustion or resentment towards others.

Promoting Personal Growth

- Boundaries create space for personal growth and self-discovery by allowing you to explore your interests, passions, and goals without undue influence or interference from others.

- They encourage you to prioritize self-development and pursue opportunities for learning and self-improvement, enhancing your sense of fulfillment and purpose.

Enhancing Self-Esteem

- Maintaining boundaries reinforces feelings of self-worth and self-esteem by affirming your right to assert your needs and preferences.
- It sends a message to yourself and others that you value and prioritize your well-being, contributing to a positive self-concept and confidence in your worthiness.

Setting Clear Expectations

- Boundaries help set clear expectations for behavior and interactions in relationships, reducing misunderstandings, conflicts, and disappointments.
- They provide a framework for healthy communication and conflict resolution, fostering greater harmony and trust in relationships.

By understanding and asserting healthy boundaries, you affirm your self-worth and prioritize your well-being, leading to healthier relationships, greater personal autonomy, and enhanced emotional resilience.

Recognizing and Communicating Your Needs

Recognizing and communicating your needs is essential for maintaining healthy relationships, advocating for yourself, and nurturing your well-being. *Here's how you can effectively identify and express your needs:*

Self-Reflection

- Take time to reflect on your feelings, thoughts, and experiences to identify your needs.
- Pay attention to physical sensations, emotions, and internal cues that signal unmet needs.

Identify Core Needs

- Determine your core emotional, physical, and psychological needs, such as safety, belonging, respect, autonomy, and connection.
- Consider both practical needs (e.g., food, shelter, sleep) and emotional needs (e.g., validation, support, understanding).

Acknowledge Feelings and Emotions

- Validate your feelings and emotions as indicators of unmet needs.
- Instead of dismissing or suppressing your feelings, acknowledge them as important signals that require attention and validation.

Practice Self-Compassion

- Be kind and compassionate towards yourself as you identify and acknowledge your needs.
- Recognize that it's natural and valid to have needs, and you deserve to have them met.

Use "I" Statements

- When communicating your needs to others, use assertive and non-confrontational language.

- Start your statements with "I" to express your feelings, preferences, and desires without blaming or criticizing others.

Be Specific and Concrete

- Clearly articulate your needs in specific and concrete terms, avoiding vague or ambiguous language.
- Provide examples or suggestions to help others understand what you're asking for.

Set Boundaries

- Establish boundaries to protect your needs and prevent others from infringing upon them.
- Clearly communicate your boundaries to others and assertively enforce them when necessary.

Practice Active Listening

- Listen actively to your own needs by tuning in to your thoughts, feelings, and bodily sensations.
- Listen attentively to others when they express their needs, showing empathy and understanding.

Ask for Support

- Reach out to trusted friends, family members, or professionals for support and guidance in identifying and addressing your needs.
- Seek out resources, such as self-help books or online forums, that provide strategies for meeting your needs.

Negotiate and Compromise

- Be open to negotiation and compromise when communicating your needs in relationships.
- Recognize that others may have different needs and perspectives, and strive to find mutually satisfying solutions.

Practice Assertiveness

- Assertively advocate for your needs without being passive or aggressive.
- Use confident body language, maintain eye contact, and speak clearly and directly when expressing your needs.

By recognizing and effectively communicating your needs, you empower yourself to build fulfilling relationships, prioritize your well-being, and live authentically according to your values and desires.

Strategies for Establishing and Maintaining Healthy Boundaries

Establishing and maintaining healthy boundaries is essential for maintaining self-respect, preserving personal well-being, and fostering healthy relationships. *Here are some strategies to help you set and maintain boundaries effectively:*

Self-Awareness

- Take time to reflect on your values, needs, and limits to understand what boundaries are important to you.
- Pay attention to your feelings and physical sensations as indicators of when your boundaries are being crossed.

Identify Boundaries

- Determine which areas of your life require boundaries, such as relationships, work, personal space, time, and emotions.
- Consider both external boundaries (physical and environmental) and internal boundaries (emotional and psychological).

Communicate Clearly

- Clearly communicate your boundaries to others in a respectful and assertive manner.
- Use "I" statements to express your needs and preferences, such as "I need…" or "I prefer…"
- Be direct and specific about what behavior is acceptable or unacceptable to you.

Enforce Boundaries

- Consistently enforce your boundaries by following through with consequences when they are violated.
- Be firm and assertive in upholding your boundaries, even if it may be uncomfortable or met with resistance.

Set Limits

- Set limits on the time, energy, and resources you are willing to invest in certain activities, relationships, or obligations.
- Prioritize your own well-being and needs by saying "no" when necessary, without feeling guilty or obligated to explain yourself.

Practice Self-Care

- Prioritize self-care practices that help you recharge, replenish your energy, and maintain balance in your life.
- Allocate time for activities that bring you joy, relaxation, and fulfillment, without feeling guilty for prioritizing yourself.

Be Consistent

- Consistently enforce your boundaries across different situations and with various individuals.
- Avoid making exceptions or compromising your boundaries to accommodate others' needs or desires.

Seek Support

- Surround yourself with supportive individuals who respect and uphold your boundaries.
- Seek guidance from trusted friends, family members, or professionals if you need help establishing or maintaining boundaries.

Practice Assertiveness

- Develop assertiveness skills to confidently communicate and assert your boundaries without being aggressive or passive.
- Use confident body language, maintain eye contact, and speak calmly and directly when expressing your needs.

Regularly Evaluate and Adjust

- Regularly evaluate your boundaries to ensure they remain aligned with your values, needs, and goals.
- Be willing to adjust your boundaries as circumstances change or as

you gain clarity about what is important to you.

By implementing these strategies, you can establish and maintain healthy boundaries that support your well-being, foster respectful relationships, and empower you to live authentically according to your values and priorities.

6

Embracing Self-Care

P*rioritizing Physical and Mental Well-Being*

Prioritizing physical and mental well-being is essential for maintaining overall health, resilience, and quality of life. *Here are some strategies to help you prioritize both aspects of your well-being:*

Physical Well-Being

Regular Exercise

- Engage in regular physical activity that you enjoy, such as walking, jogging, swimming, yoga, or dancing.
- Aim for at least 150 minutes of moderate-intensity exercise per week, or 75 minutes of vigorous-intensity exercise.

Healthy Eating Habits

- Maintain a balanced diet rich in fruits, vegetables, whole grains, lean proteins, and healthy fats.

- Limit processed foods, sugary snacks, and excessive consumption of alcohol or caffeine.

Adequate Sleep

- Prioritize sleep by aiming for 7-9 hours of quality sleep each night.
- Establish a consistent sleep schedule, create a relaxing bedtime routine, and create a conducive sleep environment.

Stress Management

- Practice stress-reduction techniques such as deep breathing, meditation, mindfulness, or progressive muscle relaxation.
- Identify sources of stress in your life and develop coping strategies to manage them effectively.

Regular Health Check-ups

- Schedule regular check-ups with your healthcare provider for preventive screenings, vaccinations, and health assessments.
- Monitor your blood pressure, cholesterol levels, and other health indicators regularly.

Hydration

- Stay hydrated by drinking an adequate amount of water throughout the day.
- Limit consumption of sugary beverages and opt for water, herbal tea, or infused water instead.

Mental Well-Being

Self-Care Practices

Engage in activities that promote relaxation, pleasure, and self-nurturance, such as reading, taking a bath, spending time in nature, or practicing hobbies.

Mindfulness and Meditation

- Practice mindfulness meditation to cultivate present-moment awareness and reduce stress.
- Incorporate mindfulness into daily activities such as eating, walking, or engaging in conversation.

Emotional Expression

Express your emotions openly and honestly, whether through journaling, talking to a trusted friend or therapist, or engaging in creative outlets such as art or music.

Healthy Relationships

- Cultivate supportive relationships with friends, family members, and loved ones who respect and validate your feelings and experiences.
- Set boundaries in relationships to protect your emotional well-being and maintain healthy dynamics.

Seek Professional Support

- Reach out to a mental health professional if you're experiencing persistent symptoms of anxiety, depression, or other mental health concerns.
- Therapy, counseling, or medication may be helpful in managing mental health challenges.

Limit Exposure to Negative Influences

- Minimize exposure to negative news, social media, or environments that trigger stress, anxiety, or negativity.
- Set boundaries around your media consumption and prioritize activities that uplift and inspire you.

By prioritizing both physical and mental well-being, you can enhance your overall health, resilience, and quality of life. Remember that self-care is not selfish—it's essential for your health and happiness.

Developing a Self-Care Routine

Developing a self-care routine is a powerful way to prioritize your physical, emotional, and mental well-being. *Here's a step-by-step guide to creating a personalized self-care routine:*

Assess Your Needs

- Take stock of your physical, emotional, and mental well-being by reflecting on areas where you may need support or improvement.
- Consider your daily routine, stressors, and lifestyle factors that impact your overall health and happiness.

Identify Self-Care Activities

- Make a list of self-care activities that resonate with you and address your specific needs and preferences.
- Include a variety of activities that nurture your body, mind, and spirit, such as exercise, relaxation techniques, hobbies, socializing, and creative expression.

Prioritize Self-Care Practices

- Determine which self-care practices are most important to you and align with your goals and values.
- Consider how you can incorporate these practices into your daily, weekly, and monthly routine.

Create a Routine

- Develop a structured self-care routine that includes daily, weekly, and occasional activities.
- Allocate specific time slots for self-care activities in your schedule, treating them as non-negotiable appointments with yourself.

Start Small

- Begin with manageable self-care activities that are easy to incorporate into your daily routine.
- Gradually add more complex or time-intensive practices as you become more comfortable and confident in your self-care routine.

Mix and Match

- Mix and match different self-care activities to keep your routine interesting and engaging.

- Alternate between activities that energize and rejuvenate you, such as exercise and relaxation techniques.

Be Flexible

- Be flexible and adaptable with your self-care routine, allowing for changes and adjustments as needed.
- Listen to your body and mind, and modify your routine based on your evolving needs and circumstances.

Practice Mindfulness

- Approach self-care activities with mindfulness and intention, fully immersing yourself in the present moment.
- Pay attention to how each activity makes you feel and its impact on your overall well-being.

Monitor Progress

- Keep track of your self-care routine and its effects on your physical, emotional, and mental health.
- Notice any improvements or changes in your mood, energy levels, and overall sense of well-being.

Celebrate Successes

- Celebrate your successes and accomplishments in prioritizing self-care and taking steps to improve your well-being.
- Acknowledge the effort and commitment you put into caring for yourself and recognize the positive impact it has on your life.

Remember that self-care is a personal journey, and there's no one-size-fits-all approach. Experiment with different activities, listen to your body and mind, and adjust your routine as needed to ensure it meets your unique needs and preferences.

Nurturing Yourself Through Self-Care Practices

Nurturing yourself through self-care practices is a deeply rewarding way to prioritize your well-being and cultivate a greater sense of balance, resilience, and self-compassion. *Here are some nurturing self-care practices to incorporate into your routine:*

Mindful Breathing

- Take a few moments each day to practice deep breathing exercises.
- Inhale deeply through your nose, filling your lungs with air, and exhale slowly through your mouth, releasing tension and stress.

Daily Gratitude Practice

- Start or end your day by reflecting on things you're grateful for.
- Keep a gratitude journal and write down three things you're thankful for each day, focusing on both big and small blessings.

Mindful Movement

- Engage in gentle movement practices such as yoga, tai chi, or qigong.
- Focus on connecting with your body, moving with intention and awareness, and releasing tension and stress.

Nourishing Nutrition

- Eat a balanced diet that includes plenty of fruits, vegetables, whole grains, lean proteins, and healthy fats.
- Pay attention to how different foods make you feel and choose options that nourish your body and support your overall well-being.

Quality Sleep

- Prioritize sleep by creating a relaxing bedtime routine and ensuring you get 7-9 hours of quality sleep each night.
- Create a comfortable sleep environment, free from distractions and electronic devices.

Digital Detox

- Take regular breaks from screens and electronic devices to reduce stress and overwhelm.
- Set boundaries around your technology use and engage in offline activities that promote relaxation and connection.

Nature Connection

- Spend time in nature to recharge and rejuvenate your mind, body, and spirit.
- Take a walk in the park, hike in the mountains, or simply sit outside and soak up the beauty of the natural world.

Creative Expression

- Engage in creative activities that bring you joy and allow you to express yourself freely.

- Explore art, music, writing, or any other form of creative expression that resonates with you.

Social Connection

- Connect with friends, family, and loved ones who uplift and support you.
- Schedule regular social activities or gatherings to nurture your relationships and cultivate a sense of belonging.

Soothing Self-Care Rituals

- Create soothing self-care rituals that promote relaxation and well-being.
- Treat yourself to a warm bath, indulge in a massage, or simply curl up with a good book and a cup of tea.

Set Boundaries

- Establish clear boundaries in your relationships and daily life to protect your time, energy, and emotional well-being.
- Say no to activities or obligations that drain you and prioritize activities that replenish and nurture you.

Practice Self-Compassion

- Be kind and compassionate towards yourself, especially during times of difficulty or challenge.
- Offer yourself words of encouragement, support, and understanding, just as you would to a dear friend.

By incorporating these nurturing self-care practices into your routine, you can cultivate a greater sense of well-being, resilience, and self-compassion, allowing you to thrive in all areas of your life. Remember that self-care is a journey, and it's essential to listen to your body and mind and adjust your practices as needed to best support your needs and preferences.

7

Cultivating Positive Relationships

E*valuating Your Relationships*

Evaluating your relationships is an important aspect of self-care and maintaining healthy connections with others. *Here are some steps to help you assess and reflect on your relationships:*

Reflect on Your Needs

- Take time to reflect on your emotional, physical, and social needs in relationships.
- Consider what you value in a relationship, such as trust, communication, respect, and support.

Assess Communication Patterns

- Evaluate the quality of communication in your relationships, including how openly and honestly you're able to express yourself.
- Consider whether communication is respectful, supportive, and effective in resolving conflicts.

Examine Boundaries

- Assess the boundaries in your relationships, including your ability to set and maintain healthy boundaries.
- Consider whether boundaries are respected by both parties and whether they contribute to a sense of safety and mutual respect.

Evaluate Trust and Reliability

- Reflect on the level of trust and reliability in your relationships.
- Consider whether you feel confident and secure in relying on others and whether they demonstrate consistency and dependability.

Consider Support and Encouragement

- Evaluate the level of support and encouragement you receive from others in your relationships.
- Consider whether others uplift and empower you, and whether they offer encouragement during challenging times.

Assess Mutual Respect

- Reflect on whether there is mutual respect and appreciation in your relationships.
- Consider whether differences are respected, opinions are valued, and there is a sense of equality and fairness.

Reflect on Emotional Well-Being

- Assess how your relationships impact your emotional well-being.
- Consider whether you feel emotionally supported, understood,

and valued by others, and whether your relationships contribute positively to your overall happiness and fulfillment.

Evaluate Conflict Resolution Skills

- Reflect on how conflicts are handled in your relationships.
- Consider whether conflicts are addressed constructively, with empathy, understanding, and a willingness to find mutually beneficial solutions.

Assess Energy Exchange

- Reflect on the energy exchange in your relationships.
- Consider whether your relationships energize and uplift you, or whether they leave you feeling drained or depleted.

Trust Your Intuition

- Trust your instincts and intuition when evaluating your relationships.
- Pay attention to how you feel in the presence of others and whether there are any red flags or warning signs that indicate an unhealthy dynamic.

Seek Feedback from Trusted Sources

- Seek feedback from trusted friends, family members, or mentors who can offer perspective on your relationships.
- Consider their insights and observations as you evaluate and reflect on your relationships.

By evaluating your relationships through these steps, you can gain clarity and insight into the dynamics, strengths, and areas for improvement in your connections with others. Use this reflection as an opportunity to nurture and strengthen healthy relationships while also recognizing and addressing any challenges or concerns that may arise.

Surrounding Yourself with Supportive People

Surrounding yourself with supportive people is vital for your well-being and personal growth. *Here are some steps to help you cultivate a supportive network:*

Identify Supportive Individuals

- Reflect on the people in your life who consistently uplift, encourage, and support you.
- Consider friends, family members, colleagues, mentors, or community members who demonstrate empathy, understanding, and genuine care.

Assess Relationship Dynamics

- Evaluate the quality of your relationships and how they impact your well-being.
- Consider whether the people in your life offer positive reinforcement, validation, and emotional support.

Communicate Your Needs

- Express your needs and boundaries openly and honestly with supportive individuals.

- Communicate what you need from them in terms of emotional support, encouragement, and understanding.

Seek Out Like-Minded Communities

- Join groups, clubs, or organizations that align with your interests, values, and goals.
- Surround yourself with people who share similar passions and aspirations, providing a sense of belonging and camaraderie.

Nurture Existing Relationships

- Invest time and effort in nurturing and strengthening existing relationships.
- Prioritize spending quality time with supportive individuals, whether through regular conversations, shared activities, or meaningful experiences.

Set Boundaries

- Establish clear boundaries in your relationships to protect your well-being and preserve healthy dynamics.
- Communicate your boundaries respectfully and assertively, and enforce them when necessary.

Be Selective

- Be selective about the people you allow into your inner circle.
- Surround yourself with individuals who uplift and inspire you, and minimize contact with those who drain your energy or undermine your self-esteem.

Offer Support in Return

- Be a supportive friend and ally to others in your network.
- Offer a listening ear, words of encouragement, and practical assistance when needed, fostering reciprocal relationships built on trust and mutual support.

Cultivate Empathy and Understanding

- Cultivate empathy and understanding in your interactions with others.
- Seek to understand their perspectives, validate their experiences, and offer compassion and support without judgment.

Practice Gratitude

- Express gratitude for the supportive people in your life and the positive impact they have on your well-being.
- Let them know how much you appreciate their presence, encouragement, and friendship.

By surrounding yourself with supportive people who uplift and empower you, you can create a nurturing environment that fosters personal growth, resilience, and well-being. Invest in these relationships and prioritize those who contribute positively to your life journey.

Communicating Effectively and Assertively

Communicating effectively and assertively is essential for expressing your needs, setting boundaries, and fostering healthy relationships. *Here are some strategies to help you communicate assertively:*

Use "I" Statements

- Start your statements with "I" to express your feelings, thoughts, and needs without blaming or accusing others.
- For example, instead of saying, "You never listen to me," say, "I feel unheard when I don't feel listened to."

Be Clear and Specific

- Clearly articulate your message and be specific about what you're asking for or expressing.
- Avoid vague language or ambiguous statements that can lead to misunderstandings.

Express Yourself Calmly

- Maintain a calm and composed demeanor when communicating assertively.
- Avoid raising your voice, using aggressive body language, or becoming overly emotional.

Use Active Listening

- Practice active listening by paying attention to what others are saying without interrupting or judging.
- Reflect back what you've heard to ensure understanding and validate the other person's perspective.

Validate Emotions

- Acknowledge the emotions of both yourself and the other person involved in the conversation.

- Validate their feelings, even if you disagree with their perspective, to demonstrate empathy and understanding.

Stick to the Facts

- Focus on presenting the facts of the situation rather than making assumptions or generalizations.
- Provide evidence or examples to support your points, allowing for a more objective discussion.

Practice Empathy

- Put yourself in the other person's shoes and consider their perspective and feelings.
- Show empathy and understanding towards their experiences and viewpoints, even if you don't agree with them.

Set and Enforce Boundaries

- Clearly communicate your boundaries and limits in a firm and assertive manner.
- Use assertive language to enforce your boundaries if they are not respected, without becoming aggressive or passive.

Use Assertive Body Language

- Pay attention to your body language, posture, and facial expressions when communicating assertively.
- Maintain eye contact, stand or sit upright, and use gestures that convey confidence and assertiveness.

Practice Self-Confidence

- Cultivate self-confidence and self-esteem to assert yourself effectively in conversations.
- Believe in the validity of your feelings, thoughts, and needs, and communicate them with conviction and assurance.

Practice, Practice, Practice

- Like any skill, assertive communication improves with practice.
- Start with low-stakes situations and gradually work your way up to more challenging conversations, gaining confidence along the way.

By practicing assertive communication, you can express yourself effectively, set boundaries, and build healthier and more fulfilling relationships based on mutual respect and understanding. Remember that assertiveness is about advocating for yourself while also considering the needs and feelings of others.

8

Overcoming Obstacles

A*ddressing Common Challenges on the Journey to Self-Worth*

Addressing common challenges on the journey to self-worth is crucial for overcoming obstacles and fostering personal growth and resilience. *Here are some common challenges and strategies to address them:*

Negative Self-Talk

- Challenge negative self-talk by replacing self-critical thoughts with more compassionate and realistic ones.
- Practice self-compassion and kindness towards yourself, acknowledging your worth and inherent value.

Comparison and Envy

- Shift your focus from comparing yourself to others to focusing on your own journey and progress.
- Celebrate your unique strengths, accomplishments, and experi-

ences, recognizing that everyone's path is different.

Perfectionism

- Embrace imperfection and accept that making mistakes is a natural part of the learning and growth process.
- Set realistic goals and standards for yourself, focusing on progress rather than perfection.

Fear of Failure

- Reframe failure as an opportunity for growth and learning rather than a reflection of your worth.
- Embrace a growth mindset, recognizing that setbacks and challenges can lead to valuable insights and personal development.

Low Self-Esteem

- Challenge negative beliefs about yourself by identifying evidence that contradicts them.
- Engage in activities that boost your self-esteem, such as pursuing hobbies, setting and achieving goals, and receiving positive feedback.

People-Pleasing

- Practice setting boundaries and saying no to requests or demands that are not in alignment with your needs or values.
- Prioritize self-care and self-respect, recognizing that your well-being is important and deserving of attention.

Past Trauma or Adversity

- Seek support from a therapist or counselor to process past trauma or adversity and develop coping strategies.
- Practice self-compassion and forgiveness towards yourself, recognizing that you deserve healing and acceptance.

Lack of Self-Awareness

- Engage in self-reflection and introspection to deepen your understanding of yourself, including your values, strengths, and areas for growth.
- Seek feedback from trusted friends, family members, or mentors to gain insight into how others perceive you.

Social Isolation

- Cultivate supportive relationships with friends, family, or community members who uplift and validate you.
- Seek out social activities or groups that align with your interests and values, fostering a sense of connection and belonging.

Imposter Syndrome

- Recognize that feelings of inadequacy or fraudulence are common and often unfounded.
- Focus on your accomplishments, skills, and qualifications, acknowledging your competence and expertise.

Resistance to Change

- Embrace change as an opportunity for growth and self-discovery, even if it feels uncomfortable or challenging.
- Break goals down into smaller, manageable steps and celebrate progress along the way.

By addressing these common challenges with compassion, self-awareness, and resilience, you can navigate the journey to self-worth with greater ease and confidence, ultimately cultivating a deeper sense of self-acceptance, value, and fulfillment. Remember that progress may be gradual, and it's okay to seek support from others when needed.

Strategies for Dealing with Setbacks and Failures

Dealing with setbacks and failures is a natural part of life, and how we respond to them can significantly impact our well-being and growth. *Here are some strategies to help you navigate setbacks and failures effectively:*

Practice Self-Compassion

- Be kind and understanding towards yourself when facing setbacks or failures.
- Treat yourself with the same level of compassion and support that you would offer to a friend in a similar situation.

Reframe Failure as Learning

- View failure as an opportunity for growth and learning rather than a reflection of your worth or abilities.
- Identify lessons and insights that can be gained from the experience, helping you to improve and move forward.

Maintain Perspective

- Put setbacks and failures into perspective by considering the bigger picture.
- Recognize that setbacks are temporary and do not define your overall progress or potential for success.

Focus on What You Can Control

- Focus your energy on aspects of the situation that you can control, such as your attitude, effort, and response.
- Let go of factors that are beyond your control and instead channel your efforts into productive actions.

Seek Support

- Reach out to friends, family members, or mentors for support and encouragement during challenging times.
- Share your experiences and feelings with trusted individuals who can offer empathy, perspective, and guidance.

Practice Resilience

- Cultivate resilience by bouncing back from setbacks with perseverance and determination.
- Embrace setbacks as opportunities to strengthen your resilience muscles and build emotional fortitude.

Set Realistic Expectations

- Set realistic expectations for yourself and accept that setbacks and failures are a natural part of the journey towards success.

- Adjust your goals and plans as needed, taking into account the lessons learned from past experiences.

Celebrate Progress

- Celebrate small victories and progress, even in the face of setbacks or failures.
- Acknowledge your efforts and accomplishments, no matter how small, and recognize the courage it takes to persevere.

Practice Problem-Solving

- Approach setbacks and failures as opportunities to problem-solve and find creative solutions.
- Break down the challenge into smaller, manageable steps and brainstorm potential strategies for overcoming obstacles.

Stay Optimistic

- Maintain a positive outlook and believe in your ability to overcome setbacks and achieve your goals.
- Cultivate optimism by focusing on possibilities, strengths, and opportunities for growth.

Take Breaks When Needed

- Allow yourself time to rest and recharge when facing setbacks or failures.
- Taking breaks can help you gain perspective, recharge your energy, and approach challenges with renewed vigor.

By implementing these strategies, you can navigate setbacks and failures with resilience, grace, and determination, ultimately using them as stepping stones towards personal growth and success. Remember that setbacks are not the end of the road but rather opportunities for redirection and growth.

Building Resilience and Persistence

Building resilience and persistence is essential for navigating life's challenges and achieving long-term success and well-being. *Here are some strategies to help you strengthen these qualities:*

Cultivate a Growth Mindset

- Embrace a growth mindset, believing that your abilities and intelligence can be developed through effort and perseverance.
- View challenges and setbacks as opportunities for learning and growth rather than fixed limitations.

Set Realistic Goals

- Set clear, achievable goals that challenge you to stretch beyond your comfort zone while remaining realistic and attainable.
- Break larger goals down into smaller, manageable steps, allowing you to track progress and maintain momentum.

Practice Self-Compassion

- Treat yourself with kindness and understanding, especially during times of difficulty or failure.
- Practice self-compassion by acknowledging your efforts, accepting

imperfections, and offering words of encouragement to yourself.

Develop Problem-Solving Skills

- Enhance your problem-solving skills by approaching challenges with a systematic and solution-focused mindset.
- Break down problems into manageable components, brainstorm potential solutions, and take proactive steps to address them.

Cultivate Optimism

- Cultivate optimism by focusing on positive aspects of situations, even in the face of adversity.
- Challenge negative thinking patterns and reframe setbacks as temporary obstacles on the path to success.

Seek Support

- Build a strong support network of friends, family members, mentors, and colleagues who can offer guidance, encouragement, and perspective during challenging times.
- Reach out for help when needed and be open to receiving support from others.

Develop Coping Strategies

- Identify healthy coping strategies that help you manage stress, regulate emotions, and maintain resilience in the face of adversity.
- Practice relaxation techniques, mindfulness, exercise, or creative outlets that promote emotional well-being.

Learn from Failure

- Embrace failure as a natural part of the learning and growth process.
- Extract lessons and insights from past failures, using them to inform future decisions and actions.

Persist in the Face of Obstacles

- Cultivate persistence by remaining determined and focused on your goals, even when faced with challenges or setbacks.
- Develop a "never give up" attitude, persisting in the pursuit of your dreams despite obstacles or setbacks along the way.

Celebrate Progress

- Celebrate small victories and milestones along your journey, recognizing the progress you've made and the efforts you've invested.
- Acknowledge your resilience and persistence, honoring the strength and determination it takes to overcome challenges.

Practice Adaptability

- Develop adaptability by remaining flexible and open to change in response to evolving circumstances.
- Embrace uncertainty as an opportunity for growth and innovation, adapting your goals and strategies as needed to navigate changing environments.

By incorporating these strategies into your life, you can build resilience and persistence, empowering you to overcome obstacles, bounce back from setbacks, and achieve your goals with confidence and determination. Remember that resilience and persistence are skills that can be developed and strengthened over time through intentional practice and effort.

9

Embracing Your Authentic Self

elebrating Your Uniqueness

Celebrating your uniqueness is a powerful way to cultivate self-love, confidence, and a sense of fulfillment. *Here are some strategies to help you embrace and celebrate your individuality:*

Practice Self-Acceptance

- Embrace all aspects of yourself, including your strengths, weaknesses, quirks, and imperfections.
- Recognize that your uniqueness adds richness and depth to your life and the world around you.

Identify Your Strengths and Talents

- Take time to reflect on your strengths, talents, and abilities.
- Acknowledge your unique skills and qualities, and celebrate the ways in which they contribute to your success and happiness.

Express Yourself Authentically

- Express yourself authentically by honoring your values, passions, and interests.
- Allow yourself to be true to who you are, rather than conforming to others' expectations or societal norms.

Celebrate Your Accomplishments

- Celebrate your achievements and milestones, no matter how big or small.
- Take pride in your accomplishments and the hard work and effort you've invested to reach your goals.

Embrace Your Differences

- Embrace the aspects of yourself that make you unique, whether it's your background, culture, beliefs, or identity.
- Celebrate diversity and recognize the beauty in individuality, both within yourself and others.

Surround Yourself with Supportive People

- Surround yourself with friends, family members, and mentors who appreciate and celebrate your uniqueness.
- Seek out relationships and communities where you feel accepted, valued, and understood for who you are.

Engage in Self-Expression

- Explore different forms of self-expression, such as art, music,

writing, or fashion.
- Use creative outlets to express your thoughts, feelings, and identity in unique and meaningful ways.

Challenge Comparison

- Avoid comparing yourself to others and focus instead on your own journey and growth.
- Recognize that everyone's path is different, and there is beauty in diversity and individuality.

Practice Self-Celebration

- Take time to celebrate yourself and your uniqueness on a regular basis.
- Treat yourself to small indulgences or activities that bring you joy and make you feel special.

Spread Positivity

- Share your uniqueness with the world by spreading positivity and kindness.
- Use your unique perspective and voice to inspire and uplift others, celebrating their individuality as well.

Reflect on Your Journey

- Reflect on your personal journey and the experiences that have shaped you into the person you are today.
- Appreciate the growth and learning that has occurred along the way, celebrating the resilience and strength you've demonstrated.

By embracing and celebrating your uniqueness, you can cultivate a deeper sense of self-love, confidence, and authenticity, allowing you to live fully and authentically as your truest self. Remember that you are worthy of love and celebration simply for being who you are.

Honoring Your Values and Beliefs

Honoring your values and beliefs is essential for living a fulfilling and authentic life aligned with your true self. *Here are some strategies to help you honor your values and beliefs:*

Identify Your Core Values

- Reflect on what matters most to you in life, such as honesty, integrity, compassion, or freedom.
- Identify your core values by considering the principles and qualities that guide your decisions and actions.

Clarify Your Beliefs

- Clarify your beliefs by examining your thoughts, attitudes, and convictions about yourself, others, and the world.
- Consider the sources of your beliefs, including your upbringing, culture, experiences, and personal reflections.

Live Authentically

- Align your actions and behaviors with your values and beliefs, living authentically and with integrity.
- Be true to yourself and honor your inner voice, even when it may be challenging or unpopular.

Set Goals in Alignment with Your Values

- Set goals and priorities that reflect your values and contribute to your sense of purpose and fulfillment.
- Consider how your goals align with your values and whether they support your vision for a meaningful life.

Make Decisions Consciously

- Make decisions consciously by considering how they align with your values and beliefs.
- Take time to reflect on the potential consequences of your decisions and whether they are in line with your principles.

Practice Self-Reflection

- Engage in regular self-reflection to deepen your understanding of your values and beliefs.
- Journaling, meditation, or quiet contemplation can help you connect with your inner truth and wisdom.

Set Boundaries

- Set boundaries that honor your values and protect your well-being and integrity.
- Communicate your boundaries assertively and enforce them with compassion and self-respect.

Seek Alignment in Relationships

- Surround yourself with people who respect and honor your values and beliefs.

- Cultivate relationships that support your growth and authenticity, where your values are acknowledged and upheld.

Stand Up for What You Believe In

- Advocate for causes and issues that are important to you, standing up for what you believe in with courage and conviction.
- Use your voice and influence to effect positive change in your community and the world.

Practice Mindfulness

- Practice mindfulness to stay grounded and connected to your values and beliefs in the present moment.
- Notice when your actions or decisions stray from your values and gently guide yourself back to alignment.

Seek Support and Guidance

- Seek support and guidance from mentors, counselors, or spiritual leaders who can help you navigate challenges and stay true to your values.
- Surround yourself with a supportive community of like-minded individuals who share your beliefs and provide encouragement and validation.

By honoring your values and beliefs, you can live a life of authenticity, purpose, and meaning, guided by principles that reflect your true essence and aspirations. Remember that your values and beliefs are unique to you, and it's important to honor and respect them as you navigate your journey through life.

Living Authentically and Unapologetically

Living authentically and unapologetically is about embracing who you truly are and expressing yourself fully, without fear of judgment or criticism. *Here are some strategies to help you live authentically and unapologetically:*

Know Yourself

- Take time to explore and understand yourself on a deep level.
- Reflect on your values, beliefs, passions, strengths, weaknesses, and aspirations.

Embrace Your Uniqueness

- Celebrate the qualities and characteristics that make you unique.
- Recognize that your individuality is a gift and something to be proud of.

Be True to Yourself

- Honor your inner truth and follow your heart in all areas of your life.
- Trust your instincts and intuition, even if they go against societal norms or expectations.

Set Boundaries

- Establish clear boundaries that protect your well-being and integrity.

- Say no to things that don't align with your values or bring you joy, without feeling guilty or obligated.

Speak Your Truth

- Express yourself honestly and openly, even if it means being vulnerable.
- Share your thoughts, feelings, and opinions authentically, without censoring yourself to please others.

Live in Alignment with Your Values

- Make choices and decisions that reflect your values and beliefs.
- Align your actions with your principles, even if it means taking the road less traveled.

Practice Self-Compassion

- Be kind and compassionate towards yourself, especially when facing challenges or setbacks.
- Treat yourself with the same love and understanding that you would offer to a dear friend.

Embrace Imperfection

- Let go of the need to be perfect and embrace your flaws and imperfections.
- Recognize that vulnerability and authenticity are strengths, not weaknesses.

Surround Yourself with Supportive People

- Surround yourself with friends, family members, and colleagues who accept and celebrate you for who you are.
- Build relationships with people who uplift and empower you to be your authentic self.

Take Risks

- Step outside of your comfort zone and take risks that allow you to grow and evolve.
- Trust yourself to handle whatever challenges come your way as you pursue your dreams and passions.

Lead by Example

- Inspire others to live authentically by being a shining example of authenticity and unapologetic self-expression.
- Encourage those around you to embrace their uniqueness and follow their own path with courage and conviction.

Living authentically and unapologetically is a journey of self-discovery and self-expression. By embracing who you are and living in alignment with your truth, you can experience greater joy, fulfillment, and authenticity in all areas of your life. Remember that you deserve to live your life on your own terms, without apology or explanation to anyone else.

10

Sustaining Your Journey

R*eflecting on Your Progress*

Reflecting on your progress is an important practice for personal growth and self-awareness. *Here are some steps to help you reflect on your progress effectively:*

Set Aside Time for Reflection

- Schedule regular time for reflection in your routine, whether it's daily, weekly, or monthly.
- Create a quiet and comfortable space where you can focus and delve into your thoughts and experiences.

Review Your Goals

- Begin by reviewing the goals you've set for yourself, both short-term and long-term.
- Consider whether you've made progress towards your goals and whether they are still aligned with your values and aspirations.

Celebrate Achievements

- Take time to celebrate your achievements and milestones, no matter how small.
- Acknowledge the progress you've made and the hard work and effort you've invested to reach your goals.

Identify Areas for Improvement

- Reflect on areas where you've faced challenges or setbacks and consider what you've learned from these experiences.
- Identify areas for improvement and growth, setting intentions for how you can continue to evolve and develop.

Recognize Patterns and Trends

- Look for patterns and trends in your behavior, thoughts, and emotions.
- Consider whether there are recurring themes or habits that are contributing to your progress or hindering your growth.

Express Gratitude

- Cultivate an attitude of gratitude by reflecting on the blessings and opportunities in your life.
- Take time to express gratitude for the people, experiences, and resources that have supported you on your journey.

Assess Your Well-Being

- Reflect on your overall well-being, including your physical, mental, emotional, and spiritual health.

- Consider whether you're taking care of yourself adequately and whether there are areas where you could prioritize self-care and self-compassion.

Adjust Your Course

- Based on your reflections, consider whether any adjustments or course corrections are needed in your goals or plans.
- Be open to adapting and evolving as you gain new insights and perspectives on your journey.

Seek Feedback

- Seek feedback from trusted friends, family members, mentors, or colleagues who can offer valuable insights and perspectives.
- Consider their observations and suggestions as you reflect on your progress and areas for growth.

Set Intentions for the Future

- Based on your reflections, set intentions for how you'd like to move forward in the future.
- Establish clear goals and action steps that align with your values and aspirations, setting yourself up for continued progress and success.

By taking time to reflect on your progress regularly, you can gain valuable insights into your journey, celebrate your achievements, and identify opportunities for growth and development. Reflection is a powerful tool for fostering self-awareness, resilience, and personal fulfillment, allowing you to live a more intentional and purposeful life.

Creating a Sustainable Self-Worth Practice

Creating a sustainable self-worth practice involves cultivating habits and routines that support your sense of self-worth and well-being over the long term. *Here's a guide to help you establish a sustainable self-worth practice:*

Set Clear Intentions

Start by clarifying your intentions for building self-worth. Identify why it's important to you and what you hope to achieve through this practice.

Identify Core Values

Reflect on your core values and principles that contribute to your sense of self-worth. Consider values such as self-respect, compassion, authenticity, and resilience.

Daily Self-Reflection

Dedicate time each day for self-reflection. Reflect on your thoughts, emotions, and experiences, as well as any challenges or successes you encountered.

Practice Self-Compassion

Cultivate self-compassion by treating yourself with kindness, understanding, and acceptance, especially during difficult times or setbacks.

Set Realistic Goals

Set realistic and achievable goals that align with your values and aspirations. Break them down into smaller, manageable steps to make progress more attainable.

Celebrate Your Achievements

Celebrate your achievements, no matter how small. Acknowledge your progress and efforts, and recognize the value of your accomplishments.

Establish Healthy Boundaries

Set boundaries to protect your well-being and honor your needs. Learn to say no to activities or relationships that drain your energy or undermine your self-worth.

Practice Gratitude

Cultivate a practice of gratitude by focusing on the positive aspects of your life. Regularly express gratitude for the people, experiences, and opportunities that enrich your life.

Engage in Self-Care

Prioritize self-care activities that nurture your physical, emotional, and mental well-being. This can include exercise, healthy eating, adequate sleep, relaxation techniques, and hobbies.

Surround Yourself with Supportive People

Surround yourself with friends, family members, and mentors who uplift and support you. Seek out relationships and communities where you feel accepted and valued.

Challenge Negative Self-Talk

Challenge negative self-talk and self-limiting beliefs that undermine your self-worth. Replace them with more empowering and affirming thoughts.

Seek Professional Support

If you're struggling with low self-worth, consider seeking support from a therapist or counselor who can provide guidance, perspective, and strategies for building self-esteem.

Practice Mindfulness

Cultivate mindfulness by bringing awareness to the present moment without judgment. Mindfulness practices such as meditation, deep breathing, or mindful walking can help you develop a greater sense of self-awareness and acceptance.

Embrace Imperfection

Embrace your imperfections and recognize that they are part of what makes you unique and valuable. Let go of the pressure to be perfect and allow yourself to be imperfectly human.

Stay Committed

Stay committed to your self-worth practice, even when faced with challenges or setbacks. Consistency and perseverance are key to building sustainable self-worth over time.

By incorporating these practices into your daily life, you can cultivate a sustainable self-worth practice that strengthens your sense of value, worthiness, and confidence, empowering you to live authentically and fully. Remember that building self-worth is a journey, and it's okay to seek support and guidance along the way.

Embracing Lifelong Growth and Development

Embracing lifelong growth and development is a mindset that allows you to continuously evolve, learn, and improve throughout your life. *Here's how you can cultivate this mindset:*

Embrace a Growth Mindset

- Adopt a growth mindset, believing that your abilities and intelligence can be developed through dedication and hard work.
- View challenges, setbacks, and failures as opportunities for learning and growth rather than fixed limitations.

Set Learning Goals

- Set goals for ongoing learning and skill development in areas that interest you or align with your values and aspirations.
- Challenge yourself to step out of your comfort zone and acquire new knowledge and skills throughout your life.

Stay Curious

- Cultivate curiosity and a thirst for knowledge by exploring new ideas, perspectives, and experiences.
- Ask questions, seek out diverse viewpoints, and engage in lifelong learning opportunities, such as reading, attending workshops, or taking courses.

Reflect on Your Experiences

- Regularly reflect on your experiences, insights, and lessons learned along your journey.
- Take time to assess your progress, celebrate your successes, and identify areas for growth and improvement.

Seek Feedback

- Seek feedback from trusted mentors, peers, or colleagues who can provide valuable insights and perspectives on your strengths and areas for development.
- Be open to constructive criticism and use it as an opportunity for growth and self-improvement.

Embrace Change

- Embrace change as a natural part of life and an opportunity for personal growth and transformation.
- Stay flexible and adaptable in the face of new challenges, opportunities, and experiences.

Practice Self-Reflection

- Engage in regular self-reflection to deepen your understanding of yourself, your goals, and your values.
- Consider what motivates you, what brings you joy, and what you aspire to achieve in both the short and long term.

Set Personal Development Goals

- Set specific, measurable, and achievable goals for personal development in areas such as emotional intelligence, communication skills, or leadership abilities.
- Break down larger goals into smaller, actionable steps and track your progress over time.

Celebrate Progress

- Celebrate your progress and accomplishments along your journey of growth and development.

- Acknowledge the effort and dedication you've invested in your personal growth, and recognize the positive impact it has had on your life.

Stay Open-Minded

- Stay open-minded and receptive to new ideas, perspectives, and experiences.
- Be willing to challenge your assumptions, broaden your horizons, and expand your understanding of the world around you.

Inspire Others

- Share your knowledge, insights, and experiences with others to inspire and empower them on their own journeys of growth and development.
- Be a role model for lifelong learning and personal growth, leading by example and encouraging others to pursue their passions and aspirations.

By embracing lifelong growth and development, you can cultivate a rich and fulfilling life characterized by continuous learning, self-improvement, and personal transformation. Remember that growth is a lifelong journey, and each step you take towards self-improvement brings you closer to realizing your full potential and living a meaningful and purposeful life.

11

Conclusion

R*ecap of Key Points*

Here's a recap of the key points for embracing lifelong growth and development:

Adopt a Growth Mindset: Believe in your ability to grow and develop through dedication and hard work. See challenges as opportunities for learning and growth.

Set Learning Goals: Establish goals for ongoing learning and skill development in areas of interest or alignment with your values.

Stay Curious: Cultivate curiosity by exploring new ideas, perspectives, and experiences. Engage in lifelong learning opportunities.

Reflect and Seek Feedback: Regularly reflect on your experiences, progress, and lessons learned. Seek feedback from mentors and peers to gain valuable insights.

Embrace Change: Embrace change as an opportunity for personal growth and transformation. Stay flexible and adaptable in the face of new challenges.

Practice Self-Reflection: Deepen your understanding of yourself, your goals, and your values through regular self-reflection.

Set Personal Development Goals: Set specific, measurable, and achievable goals for personal development. Break them down into actionable steps.

Celebrate Progress: Acknowledge and celebrate your progress and accomplishments along your journey of growth and development.

Stay Open-Minded: Remain open to new ideas, perspectives, and experiences. Challenge assumptions and broaden your understanding of the world.

Inspire Others: Share your knowledge, insights, and experiences with others. Be a role model for lifelong learning and personal growth.

By incorporating these key points into your life, you can cultivate a mindset of lifelong growth and development, enabling you to realize your full potential and live a fulfilling and purposeful life.

Encouragement for Continued Growth

Here's some encouragement to keep you motivated on your journey of continued growth:

You've Come So Far: Reflect on how much progress you've already made. Every step forward, no matter how small, is a testament to your strength and resilience.

Embrace Challenges: Challenges are opportunities in disguise. Each obstacle you overcome is a chance to learn, grow, and become even stronger.

Trust in Yourself: You have the knowledge, skills, and inner strength to navigate whatever challenges come your way. Trust in yourself and your ability to overcome obstacles.

Celebrate Your Achievements: Take time to celebrate your achievements, no matter how big or small. Each accomplishment is a milestone on your journey of growth.

Stay Curious: Approach life with a sense of curiosity and wonder. Stay open to new ideas, experiences, and opportunities for learning.

Be Kind to Yourself: Remember to practice self-compassion along the way. Treat yourself with kindness, understanding, and patience, especially during difficult times.

Seek Support: Don't hesitate to reach out for support when you need it. Whether it's from friends, family, mentors, or a counselor, support can help you stay motivated and focused on your goals.

Visualize Your Success: Take a moment to visualize the person you want to become and the life you want to live. Keep that vision in mind as you continue to work towards your goals.

Keep Moving Forward: Even on days when progress feels slow or setbacks occur, keep moving forward. Every step you take brings you closer to the person you aspire to be.

Believe in Your Potential: You are capable of achieving great things. Believe in your potential and never underestimate the power of your dreams and aspirations.

Remember, growth is a lifelong journey, and each day presents new opportunities for learning and self-discovery. Stay committed to your personal growth, and know that your efforts are making a difference. Keep shining brightly on your path to becoming the best version of yourself!

Final Words of Inspiration and Empowerment

As you continue on your journey of growth and self-discovery, remember these final words of inspiration and empowerment:

You are the architect of your own destiny, the author of your own story. Your life is a canvas waiting to be painted with the vibrant colors of your dreams and aspirations.

Embrace the beauty of your uniqueness and the power of your potential. You possess within you the seeds of greatness, waiting to blossom and flourish in the fertile soil of your passion and determination.

Believe in yourself, for you are capable of achieving anything you set your mind to. Trust in the wisdom of your heart and the guidance of your intuition as you navigate the twists and turns of your journey.

Cherish every moment, for life is a precious gift meant to be cherished and celebrated. Embrace the joy of living fully and authentically, embracing each experience with an open heart and a courageous spirit.

In times of doubt or uncertainty, remember the strength that lies within you. Draw upon the wellspring of resilience and perseverance that flows deep within your soul, propelling you forward with unwavering resolve.

Celebrate your successes, no matter how small, and learn from your failures, for they are but stepping stones on the path to greatness. Embrace the lessons they offer and let them guide you towards even greater heights.

Above all, never forget the incredible potential that resides within you. You are a shining star, a beacon of light in a world that is always in need of your unique gifts and talents.

So go forth with confidence and courage, knowing that you are capable of achieving your wildest dreams. The world awaits your brilliance, your creativity, and your boundless potential.

May you always walk in the light of your own truth, guided by the wisdom of your inner voice and the power of your dreams. And may your journey be filled with love, laughter, and endless possibilities.

Go forth and shine brightly, dear friend, for the world is waiting to be illuminated by the radiant light of your soul.

12

Resources

Tewari, A. (2023, August 24). *107 Highly empowering quotes to boost your Self-Worth. Gratitude - the Life Blog. Retrieved April 03, 2024, from https://blog.gratefulness.me/20-great-quotes-to-boost-your-self-worth/.*

ChatGPT. (n.d.-a). https://chat.openai.com/. Retrieved April 03, 2024, from https://chat.openai.com/.